PLEDGE OF ALLEGIANCE

TABLE OF CONTENTS

Pledge of Allegiance................3

Glossary........................22

Index..........................24

A Crabtree Seedlings Book

School-to-Home Support for Caregivers and Teachers

This book helps children grow by letting them practice reading. Here are a few guiding questions to help the reader with building his or her comprehension skills. Possible answers appear here in red.

Before Reading:

- What do I think this book is about?
  - *I think this book is about the person who wrote the Pledge of Allegiance.*
  - *I think this book is about the reasons why the United States has a Pledge of Allegiance.*

- What do I want to learn about this topic?
  - *I want to learn more about Francis Bellamy who wrote the Pledge of Allegiance.*
  - *I want to learn more about why we stand up and face the flag when we say the Pledge of Allegiance.*

During Reading:

- I wonder why…
  - *I wonder why people choose other people to make laws for them.*
  - *I wonder why we are supposed to put our right hand over our heart when we say the Pledge.*

- What have I learned so far?
  - *I have learned that "indivisible" means the country cannot be split into parts.*
  - *I have learned that by saying the Pledge of Allegiance it means I am loyal to the flag.*

After Reading:

- What details did I learn about this topic?
  - *I have learned that laws are rules created by a government.*
  - *I have learned that pride is having respect for something.*

- Read the book again and look for the vocabulary words.
  - *I see the word **pledge** on page 3, and the word **pride** on page 20. The other glossary words are on pages 22 and 23.*

*I pledge allegiance to the Flag
of the United States of America,
and to the Republic for which it stands,
one Nation under God, indivisible,
with liberty and justice for all*

PLEDGE OF ALLEGIANCE

The **Pledge** of Allegiance is a **symbol** of America.

It is a promise to the American flag and America.

It was written by Francis Bellamy in 1892.

The Pledge of Allegiance became the **official** name of the promise in 1945.

National Pledge of Allegiance Day is December 28.

Congress opens meetings with the Pledge.

State and city **government** meetings start with the Pledge.

*Honor the Texas flag;
I Pledge allegiance to thee, Texas,
one state under God, one and indivisible.*

Many public schools have students say the Pledge. Some have students also say the state flag pledge.

When saying the Pledge, stand up and face the flag.

Then place your right hand over your heart when saying the Pledge.

Each part has special meaning. "I pledge allegiance to the flag of the United States of America" means I am loyal to the flag.

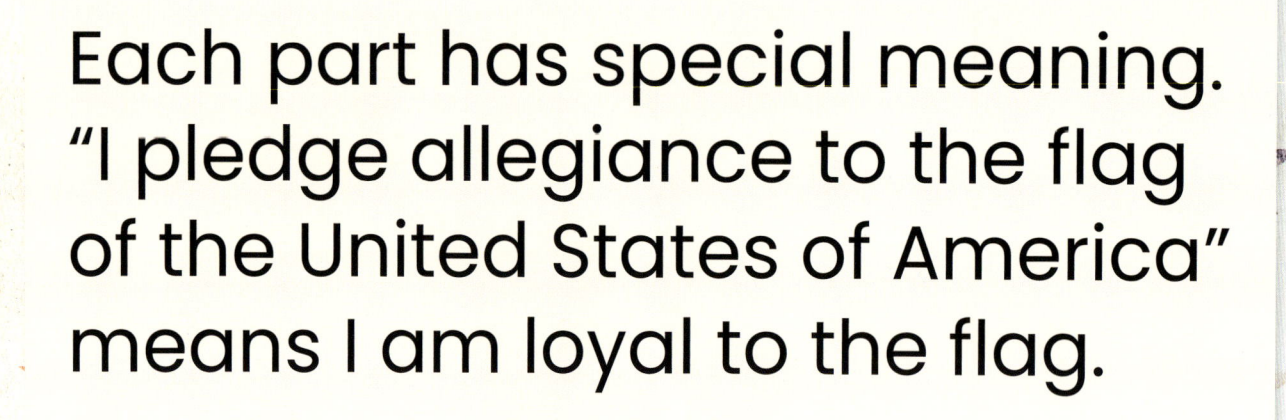

Another version written in 1885 said, "We give our heads and our hearts to God and our country; one country, one language, one flag."

"Republic" means a country where people choose others to make **laws** for them.

"Indivisible" means the country cannot be split into parts.

"Liberty" means freedom.
"Justice" is fairness.

The Statue of Liberty is a symbol of freedom. Lady Justice is a symbol of fairness.

People show **pride** for America when saying the Pledge.

The Pledge of Allegiance is an important symbol of America.

Glossary

government (GUH-vr-muhnt): The group that is in charge of an area

laws (laaz): Rules created by a government

official (uh-FI-shl): Relating to a decision made by those in charge

pledge (plej): A promise to something

pride (pride): Having respect for something

symbol (SIM-bl): A thing that represents something else

Index

America 3, 4, 14, 20, 21
Bellamy, Francis 5
flag 4, 10, 12, 14
government 8, 16
Lady Justice 19
schools 10
Statue of Liberty 19

About the Author

Christina Earley lives in sunny South Florida with her husband and son. She enjoys traveling around the United States and learning about different historical places. Her hobbies include hiking, yoga, and baking.

Written by: Christina Earley
Designed by: Kathy Walsh
Proofreader: Petrice Custance

Photographs: Shutterstock: cover: ©ArtBackground, © FabrikaSimf; ©MT511, ©dz; Title Pg: ©MT511, ©dz; Pg 4-21 ©MT511; Pg 3, 23: ©Shot Stalker; Pg 4: ©Sean Locke Photography; Pg 5: @Wiki; Pg 7, 22: ©Eliyahu Yosef Parypa; Pg 9, 22: ©Everett Collection; Pg 10: @Wiki; Pg 11: ©Tom DeCicco; Pg 12: ©Cmaxstockphoto; Pg 13: ©glenda; Pg 15: ©Bumble Dee; Pg 17: ©vectorfusionart; Pg 18: ©Skreidzeleu; Pg 19 ©Proxima Studio; Pg 21 ©Myriam Keogh; Pg 20, 23 © Dennis Owusu-Ansah

Library and Archives Canada Cataloguing in Publication
CIP available at Library and Archives Canada

Library of Congress Cataloging-in-Publication Data
CIP available at Library of Congress

Crabtree Publishing Company
www.crabtreebooks.com   1-800-387-7650

Printed in the U.S.A./072022/CG20220201

Copyright © 2023 **CRABTREE PUBLISHING COMPANY**

All rights reserved. No part of this publication may be reproduced, stored in a retrieval system or be transmitted in any form or by any means, electronic, mechanical, photocopying, recording, or otherwise, without the prior written permission of Crabtree Publishing Company.

Published in the United States
Crabtree Publishing
347 Fifth Avenue, Suite 1402-145
New York, NY, 10016

Published in Canada
Crabtree Publishing
616 Welland Ave.
St. Catharines, Ontario L2M 5V6